7 STEPS TO RELATIONSHIP MASTERY

7 STEPS TO RELATIONSHIP MASTERY

FIONA STERLING

CONTENTS

Introduction		1
1	Step 1: Understanding the Importance of Relationsh	3
2	Step 2: Developing Self-Awareness	5
3	Step 3: Effective Communication Techniques	7
4	Step 4: Building Trust and Empathy	9
5	Step 5: Conflict Resolution Strategies	11
6	Step 6: Nurturing and Sustaining Relationships	13
7	Step 7: Continual Growth and Improvement	15

Copyright © 2025 by Fiona Sterling
All rights reserved. No part of this book may be reproduced in any manner whatsoever without written permission except in the case of brief quotations embodied in critical articles and reviews.
First Printing, 2025

Introduction

In an era where technology accelerates at a breakneck pace and artificial intelligence becomes ever more sophisticated, the quality of our human interactions stands out as a beacon of connection, intimacy, and support. This book is designed to help you cultivate life-changing relationships, both personal and professional, ensuring that these connections are the best they can be.

Imagine the potential benefits of masterful interaction—whether in your workplace, family, or friendship circles. As the digital world becomes more intertwined with our daily lives, the significance of human relationships is more pronounced. Within the following pages, we offer you our heartfelt gift—a guide to refining and nurturing your ability to connect deeply with others. We also invite you to experience our trainings, which provide ongoing support and refinements to help you become a masterful relationship manager.

It's often said that when we are infants, the first thing we need is cradling, the second thing we need is holding, and the third thing we need is a relationship. This desire for connection never leaves us. People who open themselves up to relationships find that these bonds become their greatest teachers, continually inspiring personal growth and wisdom.

When relationships are flourishing, humans are at their happiest, most effective, and most creative. Conversely, when relationships falter, they can become profound sources of pain and distress. Therefore, mastering the art of relationships is essential for leading a life filled with love, joy, and fulfillment. Life itself is a creative journey, and human creativity has an evolutionary focus—realizing the infinite possibilities within our relationships.

We hope that this book will serve you well as you embark on your journey to create meaningful connections. Through understanding, empathy, and continuous improvement, you can transform your relationships into powerful, life-enhancing experiences. Welcome to the path of relationship mastery, where the evolution of your connections awaits.

CHAPTER 1

Step 1: Understanding the Importance of Relationsh

Much like the scientific method, applied relationship mastery rests on a foundational core set of steps: learning to listen, discovering how you see the world—and then understanding how someone else may perceive that world differently. It involves developing a large toolbox of communication skills, learning to resolve conflicts, setting meaningful and strategic goals, creating powerful action plans to achieve those goals, and leading others with integrity by staying true to an organization's vision and mission. These skills, while not inherently difficult at a high level, often require a significant shift in perspective and a focus on developing our current skill sets.

To create real change and impact people's lives with your ideas and vision, you need to bring others along with you. Exceptional interpersonal skills are crucial for this. Research has shown that individuals—from classrooms to boardrooms—with higher levels of interpersonal competence achieve greater success than those with only subject matter expertise. The abilities that predict future leaders are not necessarily years of education or expertise in a specific field but the capacity to make meaningful connections.

If your goal is to build a leadership or coaching practice, write a book, consult, teach, or live a truly satisfying life, relationship mastery must be the secret ingredient in your recipe. Understanding and fostering solid relationships can make your organization stand out from the competition, increase productivity, boost creativity, drive sales, reduce turnover, enhance employee engagement, and even help reduce our nation's ever-increasing healthcare costs.

Mastering relationships goes beyond the workplace; it influences every aspect of our lives. Personal relationships shape our happiness, emotional well-being, and overall life satisfaction. They provide a support system that can help us navigate life's challenges and celebrate its triumphs. The desire for meaningful connections is intrinsic to being human, and those who open themselves up to building and nurturing relationships find them to be a continual source of inspiration and growth.

As you embark on this journey to understand the importance of relationships, remember that the skills you develop will not only transform your professional life but will also enrich your personal experiences. Relationship mastery is a lifelong endeavor, and with each step, you will become more adept at creating and maintaining connections that positively impact your life and the lives of those around you.

CHAPTER 2

Step 2: Developing Self-Awareness

The growth of self-awareness has propelled human evolution in extraordinary ways. When you truly know yourself, you become more aware of limiting patterns that may have held you back. Over time, these patterns can dissolve, paving the way for new, constructive responses to life. Self-awareness naturally transforms into self-empowerment, granting you the ability to take control of your life and shape your desired experiences.

As people connect and interact, their communication and relationships improve, fostering greater trust and deeper bonds. This phenomenon reflects a fundamental law of human interactions: if you seek deeper, more fulfilling connections, prioritize sharing your reality before presenting your persona. This approach nurtures genuine connections and lays the foundation for meaningful relationships.

You are likely already aware of basic self-awareness data—your preferences, what makes you happy, your fatigue triggers, and even your big and small dreams. However, if you believe you are self-aware enough or already fully understand yourself, consider this: there might be an entire unexplored realm of self-awareness waiting for you to discover, much like an undiscovered planet called "Self-Aware Earth."

You possess the capacity to learn an immense amount about yourself by examining your behaviors and emotions. Yet, this journey requires bravery. It demands that you look beyond your ego, fears, and insecurities to uncover deeper truths about yourself. Understanding both your divine side—magical, wonderful, and unique—and your human, mortal, common side is key to forming true, just, and lasting connections with others.

As you embark on the path to self-discovery, remember that self-awareness is a continual process of exploration and growth. By embracing your full spectrum of qualities and vulnerabilities, you can achieve authentic connections and enrich your interactions with others. Your journey towards self-awareness will not only enhance your relationships but also empower you to create a life that resonates with your true self.

CHAPTER 3

Step 3: Effective Communication Techniques

Effective communication is the cornerstone of invaluable friendships and relationships. Expressing yourself with integrity and respecting others' perspectives are crucial for clear understanding. Without these elements, messages can be misinterpreted, leading to interpersonal clashes and internal disharmony. Effective communication relies equally on your sensitivity, humility, and the clarity of your thoughts.

Before crafting your sentences, examine your listening and speaking objectives. Using an appropriate vocabulary and delivering subjective messages can help eliminate misunderstandings. When friends respond positively to your probing questions, both parties lay strong foundations for successful relationships. While impulses may urge you to speak with pride, it's important to view consultations as opportunities for collaborative problem-solving. Guard against defensiveness after expressing strong opinions. Maintain open consideration and peace of mind.

Underlying self-respect and respect for others is one of life's rarest commodities: self-confidence. Confidence can fluctuate with negative experiences and emotions, blocking your energy channels. Confront your own disrespectful thoughts and restore energy balance with positive affirmations. Sending out positive thoughts helps maintain confidence, energy, and strong relationships. When self-confidence reaches an excess, humbling yourself can be beneficial.

Open communication breaks down suspicion, confrontation, and anxiety. It's the best way to achieve mutual understanding and rapidly release tension. When you have reservations, express them carefully. Be willing to listen and weigh information before making decisions. Often, the patience others show in counseling with you becomes the bond that solidifies friendships.

Effective communication fosters unity and strengthens relationships. It serves as a foundation for building trust, resolving conflicts, and creating meaningful connections. By mastering these techniques, you enhance your ability to navigate interpersonal interactions with grace and confidence, ultimately leading to more fulfilling and harmonious relationships.

CHAPTER 4

Step 4: Building Trust and Empathy

Building trust and empathy after collecting the facts involves asking the minimum number of questions needed to understand the other person's perspective. By asking questions that encourage the other person to delve deeper into their thoughts and feelings, you help establish the foundation of their communication without engaging in a thorough analysis. For example, if your child shows you a report card with poor grades, instead of asking detailed questions about their math test, such as "What was your grade on the math test?" or "Did you read the instructions correctly?", ask, "How did you feel when you saw you got a 50 on your math exam?"

Being present is crucial. When the person on the other end of the conversation feels you're not rushing them to find a solution, but rather that you're there to support them in figuring things out on their own, this kind of patience and kindness is interpreted as an open invitation to communicate. Moreover, you give them the space to build on their responses, which can lead to them finding solutions independently. Even if they're not heading towards a solution, your presence allows them to discuss other topics. By creating a nonthreatening and non-judgmental atmosphere, you show that you are truly aware of their feelings, which fosters trust.

This approach draws from Michael Bungay Stanier's work on overcoming overwhelm. Stanier emphasized that empathy is key to alleviating overwhelm. When you understand another person's perspective and share their burden, the effort required to reach an agreement or help them diminishes significantly. When someone feels safe with you, it signifies that they trust you. Building trust and empathy creates a win-win situation for any relationship.

CHAPTER 5

Step 5: Conflict Resolution Strategies

Building an environment of trust and challenging one another to engage in creative conflicts is crucial for seeking the truth. This concept is exemplified by David Kelley in his book, *Creative Confidence*. To navigate conflict resolution effectively, follow these steps:

1. **Define Each Other's Perspective**: Acknowledge that everyone has their own version of truth, and often, these truths are shared in private. Understanding these perspectives is the first step towards resolution.
2. **Work from the Same Territory**: Utilize two key tools:
   - **Neural Mirroring**: This technique calms participants and synchronizes their interactions, fostering a more cohesive discussion.
   - **Supportive Skepticism**: As defined by Carl Sagan, this involves challenging and exploring assumptions to create a synthesis of ideas.
3. **Request a Pause**: When conflicts escalate, ask for a pause. Express gratitude for the break, take some time to cool off, and continue the discussion afterward. Suggest resuming the con-

versation in private to strengthen the discussion and promote a creative exchange.

It's essential to seek first to understand, then to be understood. This process is not easy, but its benefits are profound and enduring. Before taking any step, determine whether the disagreement is emotional (stemming from strong opinions) or creative (focused on the importance and emphasis of opinions).

If you are involved in creative discussions about objectives, strategies, projects, goals, etc., you are contributing to the vitality of the team. Creative conflicts transcend individual perspectives to enhance this vitality. In contrast, strong emotional conflicts may intensify your participation, affirmation, or point of view, leading to either increased advocacy for your position or a withdrawal from it.

Effective conflict resolution also relies on open communication and mutual respect. When conflicts arise, approach them with a mindset of collaboration rather than confrontation. By building trust and demonstrating empathy, you create an environment where constructive conflicts can lead to innovative solutions and stronger relationships.

Remember, unity is strength. Embracing diverse perspectives and working together to resolve conflicts can lead to greater understanding and more effective teamwork. As you develop these strategies, you will enhance your ability to navigate conflicts with grace and confidence, ultimately leading to more harmonious and productive relationships.

CHAPTER 6

Step 6: Nurturing and Sustaining Relationships

Strengthening character and developing a relationship require keeping faith with another person, showing up for them, and defending them even when they are not present. It's easy to break a relationship and give up, but true courage, strength, and character lie in maintaining faith and working continuously to bring out the best in others. True love is what nurtures and sustains a person.

Often, we may not understand why someone behaves in a certain way. It's not our place to judge or criticize; instead, we must guide them with love, enabling them to overcome their shortcomings. Ridicule and criticism will never help elevate someone above their weaknesses. When you show love to another, you nurture them.

Nurturing and sustaining positive relationships are crucial as they provide tremendous opportunities for personal growth. There is no substitute for a stable heart and mind. Once you achieve stability, you become capable of supporting everything positive in your life. This state allows you to develop and sustain the best relationships with others. Stability is essential to providing stable love and support, which nourishes the spirit within others.

Relationships based on fear are external, while relationships from the heart are internal in nature. If you truly love someone, you will help them achieve the greatest heights of which they are capable. Love has an altruistic motive that supports the growth of the being toward the divine. Where there is no effort in that direction, there is no love. In love, there is no competition, and there is no fear.

Building and sustaining relationships require consistent effort, empathy, and understanding. By nurturing these connections, you create a foundation of trust and mutual respect that can withstand the test of time. Celebrate each other's successes, provide support during challenges, and always approach interactions with kindness and patience. Remember, the effort you put into your relationships reflects your commitment to fostering meaningful and lasting connections.

CHAPTER 7

Step 7: Continual Growth and Improvement

Focusing on enhancing the care, understanding, and relationships you maintain will positively influence your career, mental, and emotional well-being. There are, however, relationships that present extreme challenges. Ms. Zefman states, "there are some extreme situations, such as family businesses, elder care, conservatorships, greater services to family with beneficiaries, or complex litigation where the personalities or issues are magnified and negative dynamics are harder to resolve."

We also encounter various relationships in our careers, friendships, and with other family members. These unfavorable relationships can frequently lead to stressful situations. It's crucial to continually develop and hone your relational skills. Specific points that are helpful include:

- "Successful Relationship Begins in You"
- "Communication Goals and Personality"
- "Civility Skills"

These areas play a substantial role in enhancing relationships. Individuals, regardless of their expertise, can benefit from valuable information and action plans based on this advice. This might serve as a simple reminder or offer advanced civil planning to strengthen relationships. Keep in mind that even the most successful individuals seek guidance across a broad spectrum of disciplines.

Throughout history, relationships of all kinds have evolved. Social and political changes have impacted our values and expectations, reflecting on the relationships and marriages we enter into. Despite an increase in the number of marriages in the United States, the divorce rate is also on the rise. The root cause? An inability to manage relationships while coping with life's pressures.

Bethany Zefman of Long Island Family & Elder Law, LTD, observes, "this downward trend has gradually become harder and harder to reverse. From an interdisciplinary perspective, I saw that practitioners in law, business, and mental health need to concentrate on their interpersonal skills."

However, according to research from the Harvard Business Review, "the most effective leaders can be ruthless, or even shrill, and are seemingly able to separate their 'inner core' identity from their daily work persona." Mastering your relationships requires effort and time, but if nurtured, these relationships can flourish to unparalleled heights in every aspect.

Investing in continual growth and improvement of your relational skills will help you navigate the complexities of relationships, both personal and professional. Embrace the journey of self-improvement, seeking knowledge and guidance from diverse disciplines. By doing so, you'll foster stronger, more fulfilling connections and create a foundation of stability and support that enhances all areas of your life.

www.ingramcontent.com/pod-product-compliance
Lightning Source LLC
LaVergne TN
LVHW092103060526
838201LV00047B/1557